FROM THE HEART

Poems of Love and Loss

JOYCE CHIU BROADBENT

MY STORY

I read psychology at the University of Hong Kong (1974 - 77) and had a successful career in market research. 1985 found me falling in love with Mike, a client from HSBC, and we married in 1990.

Nothing perfect lasts forever. In the throes of a midlife crisis, I began a spiritual quest to discover who I was behind my different roles; and in 1997, I left alone for London to train as a psychotherapist and mindfulness teacher. A year later, Mike joined me.

By 2001, life seemed complete and Mike and I had found our place in the world. We were surrounded by close friends and shared our new home with two cherished dogs and two greatly loved cats.

The year was 2004. The neurologist just dropped a bombshell. Mike has Parkinson's Disease and had to take early retirement.

By 2015, things started to unravel. My mother had a stroke and passed away in June. Returning home from the funeral in Hong Kong I found juggling my work life and caring for my ailing husband daunting.

Things became worse. Mike caught pneumonia in December and 4.5 litres of parapneumonic effusion were drained from him. The doctor warned us he would not see another Christmas. I decided to stop working.

With the support of family, friends and the medical team, Mike's iron will fought back.

The stress of caring for Mike took its toll. Mike agreed we needed help and, after some trial and error, we found a live-in carer who became part of our family. Her name is Ana.

November 29, 2016. After jumping through several hoops, Mike was given the go-ahead and underwent Deep Brain Stimulation Surgery.

A week later, when the neurologist asked Mike to get up and walk and he did, it felt like a miracle. Mike was given a new lease on life and I started working again.

Life flows in its own impenetrable way. In June 2018, Sandy, my dearest friend in Hong Kong, passed away. She was healthy, vibrant and the last person you would imagine to die of a secondary brain tumour. And Mike began to experience all the Parkinson's Disease symptoms again.

MY POEMS

To some extent, my training served me well and I started to find solace in meditation and renewed my love for poetry.

Initially, I was able to hold the present with some degree of equanimity, to notice all the chaos erupting before me that compelled me to write what I felt.

By nature a sensitive and introvert honed to adapt to my work and social life, I found it increasingly unbearable to witness first my strong, independent husband being struck down by this cruel disease, then my mother dying and latterly Sandy.

Friends and family did their best to help but often found it difficult to say the right thing. All I could do was to retreat into myself and allowed my heart to articulate my pain. Sometimes, I did not even know what I felt and when the words wrote themselves, they revealed to me what was below the surface. Writing poems became my therapy.

The nights were the worst. I kept a semblance of containment and normality during the day. Before bed, I usually meditated, to attend to myself. And this was when the words started tumbling down recording the day and making sense of the hopelessness and helplessness I was experiencing.

I never want my poems to sink into self-pity. For me, they are the cleansing of my inner world and a way to reach out to others in a similar position; that we are all in the same boat, rowing against life's currents. And through it all, love pervades.

Contents

FOR MIKE

Getting On,
Falling Off

Outside My Window

One day,

This will fade.

The branches, stark naked,

Stretching upwards in supplication,

Will be clothed in tender baby leaves.

The sun, like a playful kitten,

Will peep out of the winter duvet

Of thought-leaden clouds.

One day,

This will fade.

And if I stride, stumble, run, dance, crawl, tip toe through life,

If I fail to notice, to realize

That this will pass,

I will have lost

This day.

A Love Poem

In bed I lie awake, alert
To your laboured breathing,
To any slight movement,
To the switching on and off of lights.

Are you caught in a nightmare
Or lying awake,
Frozen and cramped
Or shaking, unable to stop?

What dreams do you chase tonight?
Or are dreams chasing you?
Clutching at the edge of a precipice,
Frozen, mid-air?

I hear a cough, a groan,
Shall I come to you,
Hold you in my arms,
Willing you to sleep with the words:
Dream of me?

Emptying

No words,
Just tears,
And a throttled sob.

Strangling my throat,
Is the memory
Of a strong man
Struck down by the enemy within,
Crawling up the stairs
Past midnight
To the relief of his bed.

'I could still be really fit,'
He raged,
'If it were not for this fucking disease.'

He grasps every second
Of normalcy
To be useful.

To toil in the garden,
To empty the conservatory,
Ready for a new one.

Is this then our task

To empty ourselves of

Illusions of our invincibility

Unwillingly,

To make way for the promise of

Something that hopefully is our salvation?

The Enemy Within

He's not a friend,
He's the enemy within,
Like a ton of players
Pinning him down,
Rendering him immobile,
Gasping for air.

He's not a friend,
He's cunning as a fox,
Swift as an eagle,
Ready for the kill.
He dodges and ducks,
Refusing to be stilled.

He's not a friend,
He's the fiercest of foes,
Cutting him down
In the most ferocious way.
He struggles to balance,
Diving for the goal.

He scores a try.
He's a winner today.

The Bell Rings

Sitting on the bed, legs crossed,
The bell rings.
Breathe, gentle breath,
And the tears tumble down,
Gasping for breath.

The sight of my beloved
Crawling on the floor,
Bowed down by the cruelty of PD.
My rock,
Reduced to this.

With dignity, he fought back,
Saying it was only fair
To share the household chores.

How long can a heart bleed
Without draining the life blood?
How long can this fierce love
Withstand the indignity of fate?

The loneliness is the worst,

No-one truly understands.

I am scared, I am scared, I am scared.

Rocked between gasps of breaths and sobbing,

I cry to my Lord,

'Help me'.

At What Price?

I do not have a monopoly on horror.
Young men in trenches,
Rats scurrying in innards of fallen comrades,
Skulls crushed inside helmets
In no man's land.

I do not have a monopoly on loss.
Countries blown apart,
Boatloads of humanity,
The young boy dead on the beach,
The girls stolen to serve as slaves.

I do not have a monopoly on struggles.
The strong man frozen in the doorway,
Humiliated by Mr Know-All the doctor.
Blood-curling scream from a nightmare,
In the dead of night.

They tell me suffering ennobles.
At what price?

The Weather Man

When the weatherman comes,
He blows hot and cold,
And tears at my veins,
And shatters my heart.

When he comes,
Nothing can hold him,
The roof is blown,
The foundation gone.

And when he comes,
Nothing makes sense.
Time flies by so slowly,
And tears dry in torrents.

When the weatherman comes,
I melt into freezing snow.

You Ask Too Much of Me

I drove down a road
Sliding into the abyss,
Eyes trained on the headlight,
Watching out for that small
Opening I call home.

When the fireworks hit the sky,
Wayfarers in funny hats
Called out greetings of
Good cheer.
I sat alone in the dead of night,
Eating a microwaved meal.

You ask me to understand
What it's like to be you,
Battling a degenerative disease,
Testing limits,
Testing mine.

Do you know what's it like,
Fighting the system,
For your life,
For mine,
Home from hospital,
On New Year's Eve?

Befriending Death

Every Day, Every Hour

Every day, every hour,
I lose a bit of you.
In a cafe by the beach,
She took me aside,
Warned me of a
Disease that will
Suck us dry.

It sucked up first your job,
Your mobility, your speech.
Your superior mind held hostage
In a decaying body.

Every minute, every second,
You leave yourself,
You leave me
With more memories
Of the man who was
And who is now no more.

Here Comes the Night

Alone again surrounded by loved ones,
Handpicked to pledge allegiance
To me through highs and lows.

It is not easy.
How can I tell them,
My tears tumble unabated,
Sitting here in the stillness of my chaos?

How can I tell them,
You have left me before you are gone,
Lost in a haze of Stellas and Cindys?

I seek refuge in a host of ways:
In books, prayers and meditation,
In writing bad poetry.

How can I tell you,
I am cast adrift
From myself, from you?

PD meds: Stellas = Stalevo; Cindys = Sinemet

My Heart in Absentia

Today.

My heart saw
Love and stuff
That was too hard to bear.

What she saw,
I'll tell you in confidence,
Please don't tell anyone.

She saw a heroic man
Disintegrating into
Millions of pieces.

My heart searched in vain
For fragments of his mobility,
His voice, his dignity.

This heart broke
With impotence
Into millions of pieces.

That is why,

I have mislaid her deliberately

With his fragments.

Today.

The Trickster

The clanging of the water pipes
Has its own rhythm
Which I know not.

In the midst of an unquiet night,
I pause and listen,
And there is silence,
Only to be caught unawares
When I feel all is well and it
Rips my peace apart.

Such is the trickster in my mind
Harsh, unyielding, unremitting,
Clamouring for attention.
And as I near life's journey end,
I pray for a God
Who will carry me home safely.

I have a Little Secret

I have a little secret, I hold it dear in me.
It weighs me with its malice, it bars me from my sleep.
The tears course down my face,
I will not let it go.

I have a little secret, a trump card in my life.
At night I dream of death,
And God's covenant in gold.
At dawn I crave my sleep to blot my life away.

I have a little secret: to go in search of death,
Befriend it, tame it, make it my own pet.
I hold the shards of fear,
In the tenderness of my heart.

I have a little secret birthed the day I woke,
With the same tears down my face,
And a murmuring of old:
One day nearing death, one more day for living.

I have a little secret, I have a little pledge:
The day he dies I will
Travel, go on cruises,
But that day I will die, that day, I will surely die.

I have a little secret, waiting in the wings,

I cannot bear the living,

I cannot bear the dying,

Life is but a stage and so is dying too.

I have a little secret,

I read other people's angst,

I taste each morsel gingerly,

And feel it in my breath.

I have a little secret.

I cry to God above:

'I tire of all your hide and seek!'

I confided with my tears.

Let Me Grieve Alone

Let me grieve alone,
Feel the pain,
The dread resolved,
The condolence received,
The mourning done.

Let me feel the tidiness
Of the loss,
A beginning and end,
Moving round rooms
Replete with you.

Let me wail alone
In your study, bedroom
With the wheelchair, recliner,
Pills, alarm bell,
A peddling bike unused, forlorn.

Let me say farewell
To my dear dear man.
You will return
A new man
Purged of the curse.

I Abdicate

Words repeat themselves,
There is nothing new in human experiences.
So what have I to offer,
But the same old story?

Winter sets in.
I fear for the health, the life of the other.
My heart pounds a slow deadening beat,
Waiting to die, waiting to live again.

The angels are here,
Ministering to us.
Yet the world still falls apart,
And nothing makes sense.

Innocence lost.
The young wife, defeated by the husband
Repeating the same mistakes as his father,
Went searching for love in another,
Abandoning her dreams, her husband, her young children.

This then is our new generation,
While the older wrestle with their past, their present, their future,
Their countries torn apart by the hard left and right, by fear.

I cannot even find privacy in my own home

Spiritual sanctity, authenticity,

And so,

I abdicate

From life.

For Sale

I wake up to the
For Sale sign
Of this house...
What else is for sale?

My conscience,
My integrity,
In exchange for
A life better lived?

Not trapped,
Not stranded,
Not waiting.
Dying.

Looking into
The abyss,
The aridity of this life,
What else can I sell?

Alienated.

Alienating.

Waiting to Die

We celebrate your birthday,
All smiles.
They talk of their kids,
All grown.
Living with them,
Not gone.

We sit,
Eating a delicious Eritrean meal
Lovingly prepared
By your Eritrean carers.
Glad to be alive,
Not dead.

They talk of their future,
Retired, retiring,
Kids finding jobs, marrying,
Having kids.
We sit,
Waiting to die.

I Pretend

I do not have a bucket list.
I stay quiet,
While friends talk of Italy:
Venice, Rome, Florence.
Inside, my heart weeps.

We sit laughing,
Drinking champagne,
While you sip your lime juice.
I imagine it was still possible
To be happy, carefree.

This NOW is not normal,
A passing nightmare.
We will wake up,
Laugh again,
And choose what wine we'll have for dinner.

I pretend.

They Tell Me

They tell me to stay strong for my husband.
I sob alone,
My cat snuggles up for company.

They tell me to share my tears with my husband.
He worries and frets,
I turn on him and my cat is confused.

They tell me to share my sorrow with others.
I do and the sorrow lessens,
Only to increase amongst those who love me.

I am alone within my bubble.
Alienated, alienating,
Wasting, wasted.

Such is the futility of well-meaning advice.
You can only understand when you are submerged in it.
And how can you?

Don't Tell Me

When you see the man you love freezing, shaking, feverish,

When he only has end of life conversations, slurring his words which you half understand,

When he sneaks out and strangers, policemen, the ambulance call you and appear at your door,

When you rush to his aid late at night and early in the morning,

When he screams from a nightmare at the dead of night,

When he adjusts his medication to be on top form seeing friends,

When you witness him collapsing after seeing friends,

When the food you cook is half eaten because he has problems swallowing,

When you make sure his friends understand what he is saying,

When you resolve everyday to remain strong, faithful, loving, even joyful,

Don't tell me to be positive, to make the best of life.

I. Am. Fine.

You ask me how I am.

The slow tortuous stream
Of anguish flows secretly.

Feel the undercurrent of sorrow,
Hear the bubbling babbling of fear,
Catch the blood of each splish splash,
Ricocheting mid-stream
Against each rock.

I put on my make-up,
Smile at you,
And say

'I'm fine.'

Aftermath

Time Out

I am taking
Time Out
From Life,
I announce to the World.

Life is better now,
Is the light
At the end of your tunnel
Blinding you?

What is wrong
That you don't realise
Life is better
Than a year ago?

Why the torrent of tears?
Why the unyielding pain?
Why the need to escape,
To hide when Life is better?

My body battered and bruised
Tightly coiled, rigid, rusted,
Has nothing more
To give.

Time Again

<u>3:35 am</u>.
Time again.
I stirred,
Swirling colours,
A palette of memories,
A heart palpitating,
Someone screaming,
Writhing on the floor
It is me.

<u>4:30 am</u>.
The birds awake.
I got out of bed,
The rock salt lamp,
Glowing pink in the room,
The darkness outside,
Lit by a single
Solar powered light,
Alone.

4:35 am

Wide awake.

I saw

An evergreen

Laden with green leaves,

Swaying softly in the lawn,

A deciduous,

Stretching bare branches,

Wordlessly up to the sky

And I wonder.

Why do we not just

Grow evergreens,

A perfect world

And be done with it?

Why do we

Grow deciduouses,

Shedding in autumn,

Skeletal in winter?

I wondered.

And I know.

The Gossamer Sweetness of Youth

Early one morning
Walking my dogs,
I saw a gentleman,
Tall, stooped, smiling,
With his lady companion.
I smiled.
What a loving couple.

He came everyday
For a walk.
One day,
The companion was another woman.
In my innocence
I thought,
'How strange.
Did his wife die
Replaced by another?'

Today.
The gentleman
Is my husband,
The companion,
His carer.

Simple Pleasures

Simple pleasures.
Watching telly together,
Waiting for the
Countdown and fireworks,
Announcing the New Year.

Simple pleasures.
A cooked meal shared,
Exchanging stories of the day,
Laughing at life's absurdities,
Putting the world to right.

Simple pleasures.
Sunday mornings,
Dogs yowling in the car,
Deer across the fields,
Hot coffee and a burger.

Simple pleasures.
Queuing in the cinema,
Popcorn and a large coke,
Walking back home,
A takeaway for dinner.

No more.

FOR FAMILY AND FRIENDS

Siblings

The Eleventh Hour

(Dedicated to Libby and Evie)

While I was showering at eleven this morning,
A shaft of sunlight struck my face, and these words came to me:

An angel of light, bursting through the storm clouds of despair,
Carries gently under her wings
The blessings of my twin sisters.

Siblings

We are leaves from the same tree,

Torn asunder and scattered,

To the far reaches of the earth.

We find roots in lands familiar and alien,

Breathe a different air,

Learn a different language,

Plant a different tree in a different soil,

And long to return to the tree that is no more.

Fragments of Love

(Dedicated to Libby)

Shaken, being chastised,
Alone, unloved,
You quietly guided me
To the clothes section,
Bought me a blue top
And a belt to match.

Many years later,
I wear them,
And wonder at
How blessed I am,
To have a sister
As amazing as you.

Ageing

October

Arriving this morning at seven,
In the most prosaic surrounding,
Performing the most prosaic tasks,
I discovered candy floss clouds,
Flecked with bits of heaven
Outside my bathroom window.

Nature opened before me,
Beckoning me to be still.
I gazed, stunned
By the majesty of the oak tree,
Stretching wing tipped leaves above,
The vines still jostling on the trellis wall,
And the leaves below
Suffused with red autumnal hues.

Summer is dying,
Giving way to my favourite month:
October.

And I will turn sixty.

The Stranger

When will I settle into this old person's face,
A face I sketched when I was but a child?
The strands of which are still here, teasing me
With its curved lips, its small nose.

A face that used to be beautiful,
Never fully acknowledged,
Self-conscious, full of angst,
How could I?

Now, the skin is loose and the colour grey,
The eye bags heavy, the wrinkles, etched.
I see my mother's face
Peering back at me.

When will I come to love
This stranger who stares back at me?

Our Time Has Passed

(Dedicated to Carol, best friend since we were five)

We sat
After the meal,
My husband left
A space for us to fill.

We poured over photos of youth,
Reminisced on ours,
And know our time has passed.

Photos of stunning young women,
Poised to conquer the world.
We want for them to embrace it as we did,
Wide-eyed innocence behind sophisticated masks.

We want for them to ride the highs and lows,
And dare to love and win and lose.
I want it for their sake,
And for ours too.

For our time has passed,
And our lives were full.
Now, we are invisible,
And wiser, more generous and sadder too.

For the time has come to mourn the loss

Of those who left us, and

The time has come for us and

So will for them too.

Loss

When Someone Dies

(Confessions of a Grieving Daughter)

I wonder if you ever experienced
The desire to be part of some other
Yet reject all asunder?

I wonder if you tremble at the brokenness within,
Then smile your smile and talk the talk,
As expected of you?

When someone close to you dies,
Someone you love
And hate,
This is how I feel.

I hate her for leaving me bereft of my illusions,
For shattering the invisible glass of myths,
For revealing the ugliness of death.

I hate her for leaving me
So scared, so angry,
So selfish, so lost.

And I love her with all the inside of me,
Now torn apart,
Pregnant with sorrows.

A Season for Remembering

How can it be
I'm sixty-four?
At my age,
My parents married me off
At thirty-five.
What have I achieved?

How can it be
I'm different
And the same?
A hopeless idealist,
An earthbound pragmatist,
Finding it difficult
To be me?

How can it be,
The life-blood created in me
Is now dried up, desiccated?
Missing my mother's cooking,
My father's moral compass.

I'm broken off
From the ones who loved me,
Their youth I never noticed,
Their youth wasted, neglected.

I can still hear her sweet singing voice
Calling my name,
I can still see his stern handsome face,
Studying me
With bemusement and pride.

How can I be
The daughter
Of this man
This woman
I love,
Long gone?

One Year Ago

Forty years ago,
She cooked me dinner,
Admonished me to study hard,
Grow into womanhood,
Not be reliant on men.

Twenty years ago,
She was in the news,
On the stage exhorting
The elderly to live fully,
The setting sun at its most brilliant.

Five years ago,
I thought she would live forever,
Her smooth unlined complexion,
Her black uncoloured hair,
So alive so alert.

One year ago,
She left us.
Our family fell apart,
Never the same again,
The will is lost.

Twilight

In the twilight of our years,
I meandered back into our youths
Of camaraderie and laughter;
Hyper-vigilance and aloneness.
I tread the land of milk and honey
Under a blanket of nails,
And long for the safety of a home.

And in my yearning,
I missed the signpost called YOUTH,
Bypassed the one named GRATITUDE.
In the twilight of my years,
I miss already the love of my mother,
Declaring: 'I am blessed. Thank you God.'

I miss her
Like a child,
As she fades away,
Leaving me
Forgotten, unloved,
An orphan.

In Death We Greet Life

(Dedicated to Phyllis, my Reiki Master)

What is death?
What is life?

Today I receive your news,
That you have not long for this world,
And you mapped out
Your plans
For what is left of your life.

In death, we greet life.
I have greeted much of life
In the past months.

In the encounter of the ugliness of death in my mother's eyes;
In the struggle with the grim reaper in my beloved's breath.

He still lives, bravely, a hero.
Now it is your turn.
And soon, mine.

Immeasurable Sorrow

(Dedicated to Sandy)

There are no words to fill this page,

Only the oppressive heat,

The whirring of an air conditioner,

The darkness of the night.

And in a split second,

I heard your voice

Calling my name 'Ah Joy!'

And I remember

Our youth again.

Hope

Waking up from a Dark Night of the Soul

Dawn, stretching her sinuous body,

Scattered rainbow hues

On an unsuspecting world.

Inspired by Constable

Can you see
The glittering diamond of
A whitewashed house,
Sparkling against the sulky sky?

Can you hear
The menacing whispers of
The skeletal trunk,
Threatening to pierce the courageous heart?

Can you spy
The turrets' shadows,
Looming heavily over the cottage small?
Is it friend? Is it foe?

Can you trust
The beckoning light,
The promise of a welcoming hearth,
A haven for the weary soul?

FOR CLIENTS AND STUDENTS

My Friend, The Poem

The Poetry Workshop

I have not come so far,
To be dragged back
To a present that
Is an illusion.

Perhaps it will be
Different this time?
Perhaps for now,
This is enough?

Ode to Poetry

I found the words I lost,

Through the passage of time,

Hop-skipping from millennium old

In poetry.

They dance sometimes two in a row,

Crossing rainbow bridges,

Gliding through vales and lakes,

Lightly toe tapping in the forest of my mind.

My Brave Clients

The Serenity Room

In the comfort of my serenity room,
Bathed in the softness of a setting sun,
You hurled invectives at me.

'What makes you better than me,
In your comfortable space,
Your comfortable chair?
You splatter me with your compassion,
You make me crawl and walk
Over hot coals for my salvation.'

Two vulnerable people,
One, offering the best of whom she is,
The other, his anguish.

Lost Souls

Here I am,
My mind full of lost souls,
My heart breaking into sad songs.

A word, a glance,
A human connection,
A subtle recognition of one
By another.

You talked of dreams,
Your pain, your dark secrets.
The little girl who longed for her daddy's permission.

The father who lied about his affairs,
The mother who made herself a martyr,
Made you complicated.

You yowled:
'You wimp,
I hate you, don't leave me.'

We are more similar than our differences:
The human endeavour to love, be loved,
Lost in the sea of shoulds and musts,
Lost in the tide of shame and guilt.

We yearn for that knowing look, that faint smile,

That says: 'I have been there.'

Learning to Fall

Today she crossed the line:
She was crass and pushy,
Not very likeable.

Proving what she secretly feared:
Wild and untameable,
Alienated and alienating,
She caused her mother grief,
And now,
More.

She was never the good one,
The sociable one.
She found solace in make-believe,
And pretended
She was the good one,
The sociable one.

And now, the chink in her armour is revealed,
And she is learning to fail,
To fall
Undeserving into the grace of God.

Let Me Understand

Let me understand you.
You talk in tongues,
Contradicting yourself,
Contradicting me.

A man born with an
Acute sense of observation and reasoning,
Straddling the inner and outer world,
A stranger to yourself.

You spoke a language not your own
To communicate with others.
You felt a sense of duty
To serve the world with your gift.

You found a voice,
And realized too late it was not your own.
At the age of fifty,
You determined to
Not sacrifice yourself anymore.

You started to speak in tongues again,
To find amidst them your own voice,
And resolve to find someone who could understand.

The Other

I am tired and sleep escapes me,
Crowded by images of the other,
Cramped together
In a sacred space.

I could not breathe,
Attempting to be too clever with words.
My soul escaped to greener pastures
Wherein lay realness and honour.

We came to this space
Hoping to meet the other
On the soul level,
And yet, I still hid under the banner
Of the therapist's imperative to be authentic.

I was not truly there,
Though I felt I was,
I was not truly naked,
Though I wish I were,

So people can still love me
For who I am,
And shame or guilt
Won't rob me of myself.

I do not want to disappear,

I do not want to be miserable

Any more.

I continue to long for God's grace.

Unforgiven

I get out of bed,
Moved by the image of a
Haunted man
Crazed by the curse of unforgiveness:

'I killed my mother,
Left her to die in agony
Without morphine.'

Now he chooses to suffer for his mother,
Tormented by the ghosts of evil creatures,
A hating god,
Pouring boiling water on his face,
Raping him, shitting on him.
He cannot sleep, cannot eat,
A husk of a soul,
In the emptiness of a psychiatric ward.

I am alone with his terror,
I cannot reach him,
I cannot even reach myself,
Doubting how I could be of help,
How he could be helped.

Will a listening God listen?
Or has He gone out to lunch?

A Spiritual Encounter

In Spite Of

In spite of

Lying here

Prone

On the reiki bed

With my wandering mind,

I receive

The nectar of God's love

In the hands

Of my students.

When I Disappear

(After a Reiki treatment)

When I disappear,
The pain that
Inhabits my body
Goes AWOL,
And my emotions discover
A land of milk and honey,
And sweetness caresses my soul.

When I disappear,
The Heaven's gates open,
And angels embrace me with silvery wings,
Whispering tenderly:
'You are loved
Always,
And loving is easy and natural.'

When I disappear,
I kiss mother earth and all that inhabits it.